Prospecting

Increase Your Income and Learn How to Always Have a Full Pipeline of People Wanting to Buy from You Using Cold Calling, Social Selling, and Email

Volume 1

By

Income Mastery

Table of Contents

Introduction

Do you know how to be successful and why some people succeed in business? This book is for you if you want to increase your income and learn to have commercial operations indefinitely from clients who want to buy in your business using different techniques and strategies. Keep reading if you are starting a business or if you have a business, but you are not generating enough sales or you generated a lot of sales and you no longer know how to sell. If you don't know what to do to get more customers, if you want to learn how to retain customers and be recommended. Read on if you want to be a successful person with increased income and indefinite business operations.

On the other hand, we will recommend the positive habits of successful people, how to limit procrastination and fight it, not let your thoughts limit you, not watch so much television, take care of your health, see what our strengths are and put together realistic lists of tasks that we can accomplish. If our to-do lists are very ambitious, the only thing we will achieve will be to become frustrated when we do not succeed in accomplishing everything. The same happens with the goals, if they are not real, we are going to get frustrated if we have had sales and have good prospects.

To be successful we must take risks, think outside the box and make that decision that will lead us to success.

It's not easy, otherwise everyone would do it and be successful. If you know your value and have the right attitude and tools, you can do it, don't be discouraged. Have you ever wondered why a person is successful? Because they don't make excuses, they don't stop calling their prospects because they say it's lunchtime, or that they'd better call them another day. It is important not to postpone what we should do and what we have been planning. Successful people don't complain either, saying they don't have time, they're stressed out, they don't respond, they're not being treated well, they're not being answered, or any other complaints or excuses they may have. They see the positive side of each situation and learn to turn them around. Successful people don't procrastinate either, you know why? Because they understand the importance of continuing to work, of searching for prospects, of replacing them, of continuing to search, of calls, of meetings, they understand the importance of the mails they send and the importance of the information and research of the company and its needs.

Are you ready to be successful and to learn everything from prospecting? This is the key to success. Even if the economy is not good, successful people never stop prospecting because they understand that doing this is the key to success. The more prospects we look for, the more fruit we will have. In this book we will talk about the importance of joint marketing efforts, that potential customers know us, the importance of following companies and having alarms like Google Alerts in case companies move, are bought by other companies, are going to have a new line of another product, among others. These events, better known as "trigger events" are the window and the difference between getting a client and not getting it. The information in the sales category is worth gold. Being informed of what is happening not only in our industry but also in our prospect industry is of paramount importance.

Chapter 1: What is a prospectus?

Do you know what a prospect is and do you know what separates a prospect from a contact in a company that is not interested and will not be interested in your product? When we talk about prospects, we are referring to potential customers. This means that they are people who could buy our products or services based on their characteristics, interests and needs. These are the people we should look for, invest our time in them, seek meetings with them and sell them the added value of our product, not just sell the product. The prospect should always feel that our product is going to make them look better at work before their boss or that it is going to help them increase sales and/or productivity of the company.

On the other hand, we must also analyze our supposed prospects and we must build a database of these people in order to build strategies around them. So, a prospect is a potential customer who could buy your product based on their position in the company, their previous purchases or the interest they have shown in companies similar to yours. Why is it important to search and work on prospects? Because we spend our time and energy better when we turn to them, we have a better chance of closing deals with prospects, that is, if we work our list and look for prospects, our chances of closing deals are higher than if we had not worked. Why? The list of customers that we may believe to be potential is very broad, the customers that are actually potential, or prospects, are smaller. Is it easy? No, it's not easy to work out a list of prospects. We must investigate, make informed decisions, see where the person works, what position they hold, in what company they work, we must investigate the company, we must communicate with prospects, etc..

Do we benefit from researching the potential customers we're going to call? Of course, we won't waste time calling and visiting or having a meeting with someone who doesn't fit my product's profile or who isn't going to buy our product. Many times we get frustrated because we feel that we are not getting answers from potential customers, but suddenly the problem is that the customers we have been contacting are not potential customers, they are customers who do not fit in with my company and are not prospects, that is, they are not going to buy my product because they do not need a product like mine.

What does success mean to you? Do you consider yourself a successful person? How do you see success and how do you see yourself? Let's start by talking about sales success, not just how we can achieve it, but how we can maintain it. It's very easy to feel comfortable if we're doing well. We must remember that we must always look for new prospects, go to meetings, try to make a name for ourselves and our company in the industry. So how do we achieve success? We cannot talk about success or how to maintain it without starting with planning, strategies and tactics. We must begin by thinking about the planning and strategies that we must develop. There is no point in selling for the sake of selling what is crazy because it is not going to be sustainable over time. We must understand how to sell and whether we are selling not only to the right people, but whether we can improve our sales. Most of us think there's only one way to do things, but it's not true. What works for one doesn't work for the other. We must keep an open mind towards all the possibilities that are presented to us.

So, what does it mean to sustain your company's success and how can we do it? First, we must start by making our long-term sales plan. Understanding our numbers is really important in order to achieve a sales plan that more closely resembles reality. We can start by reviewing our previous sales, if possible, we must have the purchases of the previous twelve months and our costs of the same time. In case our company has more time, better. Next, we must begin to analyze where our sales come from in order to classify customers. Who do our customers buy from? What distribution channels do our customers come from? What distribution channels are we using in our business? Do they have a cost? How many people do they reach? Can these distribution channels segment potential customers? This will give us an idea and help us identify sales opportunities in other channels and if we have any weaknesses.

Why aren't we selling through some specific channel and what can we do to remedy it? What is the competition doing? Do we know who they are? It is extremely important to know which companies are our competitors, what are they offering, through which distribution channels, what is their added value, and with which companies are they working? Having this information from our competitors is very valuable, knowing what they are offering their prospects, we can improve our proposal and highlight some features of our product, along with added value, so that prospects when comparing both companies decide to buy and work with us. We must review what their channels are, what they are doing on social networks and how they offer their product. This will help us to differentiate ourselves and to be able to show a product with more benefits than that of our competition. Do not forget to compare the price to see how our price is in relation to the price of our competitors.

We also need to see how many customers and prospects we have. High value customers and prospects help us sustain the company, but how many do we have and how much would it affect us if they stopped buying our product or service? When does your contract expire? What should I offer them to renew the contract? Have they had a problem with us? How have we reacted to the problem? What can we offer them? Do we have an upgrade, some additional feature or can we offer them some extra discount? Classifying customers by monetary value at this point will help us define how much effort we should make and where we should put the most effort.

Which customer is more important? To whom should I pay more attention? How much discount can I give to this particular customer? How and what can we do to avoid losing these more important customers? These questions are very necessary because they help us make informed decisions about what to offer companies to buy our product or contract our service. It is of utmost importance not to start offering a discount, we must be able to negotiate with them. Sometimes we think that the prospect will not want to pay the full price of the product and then we realize that we are wrong.

Likewise, once this classification of clients has been made, we must begin to segment them. Why is this important? In case we have different products and/or services that we can offer to different customers, the segmentation shows us which and who are the potential customers for the sale of that particular product or service. When segmenting we are taking into account different factors that will make some prospects more inclined to buy a particular type of product from us.

Also, when carrying out different campaigns or actions such as sending emails, these should be sent to the segmentation that goes according to the product in order to maximize our efforts and that these are directed to the right audience. This will maximize the chances of selling our products.

Also, if we are to make phone calls offering this particular product, this specific segmentation of customers must be made. For example, if we have a database with customers who are interested and who have purchased a particular product from us or could do so, call them, send them emails or conduct campaigns on social networks, for example, with them as segmentation is going to be more productive and will have more conversion than making these campaigns to customers who are not interested.

We have to analyse whether we are offering our full range of services to all our clients. Many times, without realizing it, we stop offering our services because we think that a client does not fit the profile and will not want them. Are you guilty of this? Do this exercise, write down everything your company has to offer. When you are communicating with a customer, even though you are offering a particular product, also tell them about the other services you offer. Not only does it serve as a recommendation to friends once they ask, this particular customer may need this additional product or service and may be looking for it at another company. Simple truth? This is also known as "up-selling", who is a potential customer who initially comes looking for a particular product or service and the seller offers additional products and he buys them.

Are you missing these opportunities? Does your sales team know they are selling it? How are they selling and how are they offering these additional products? How do they present themselves? This is very important to be able to make sales, the way you offer services and how much you know your own products and / or services can give security or distrust to the customer.

Can we make sales and increase them magically? No, we must do all the work necessary to be able to sell as much as we can to the customers we can get. We must call customers, send them emails, promotions of our products and / or services, adjust and customize the proposals sent, give them the added value of our product. Our service and treatment towards them is vital, if they get along better with us and we make their work easier, they will choose to work together instead of working with our competitor.

Actually, having prospects is quite a challenge, but it can be done. There are companies with specialized databases to send emails with the logo of our company and our promotions. This would be a good place to start, so we can feed our database, ie, our prospects and then be able to segment.

Chapter 2: Having the Right Mentality

In order to obtain results and achieve success we must always have the right mentality and attitude. Let's start with the attitude that should be positive. How is your mind? Are you more focused on the negative or are you pessimistic? You must begin to think positively, you can do this with meditation or with gratitude. Why is this so important? Because we are going to fail, but we must know how to handle defeat and take the positive side of it. This will help us make better decisions. Are we defeatist-minded? If so, we'll never risk it. It is very important to take risks and know that there is always a risk that things will not turn out as we expect, but if we never try we will never know if it works or not, right?

Read what CEOS or the world's most successful people do. How many hours do they sleep a day? What time do they get up? How did they achieve their success? Duplicate and adopt these habits. We know that most successful people get up very early and sleep early, read, play sports and are healthy. They deal with stress, have a positive attitude and dare to take risks. Adopt these habits and expect positive changes in your attitude and business. We must learn to manage stress and learn to manage our emotions. What does this have to do with mentality? Learning to manage our mind, that is, what we think, our emotions, learning to handle defeats and always seeing the positive side, we can keep motivating them and therefore keep looking for prospects, scheduling meetings and closing businesses.

Changing our mindset is not only going to improve and change the way we see our business, our family, the people around us and our lives. For example, at any given time, the success we will have will be being able to dedicate ourselves to what we want, what we like and having a flexible schedule, being our own boss. We must remember why we have begun this journey and all the benefits that hard work will bring us. Let's imitate and read the success stories of people who have been successful. Most of those stories have in common that they didn't succeed at first, but they didn't give up either, they started again and in that after a lot of effort and dedication to their business, they were successful.

It is important to be open to new strategies, new tactics and constructive criticism. There is never a single way to achieve success, we must be open to learn new ways to operate in our industry, to deal with potential customers, to look for potential customers and we must remember that this path will not be easy but it will be worth it. If we have the right mentality, we will not lose motivation, we will continue to work hard to achieve our goals. If we have a team, the fact that they see us motivated will motivate them. Regardless of whether we have many sales or few sales, we must always keep working hard and exchanging information with our collaborators.

Chapter 3: Cold calling, what are they and how do they work?

Cold calls? Does this technique still work in an age of so much technology? We think so, but those calls should be smart and we should have done some research before calling the prospect. Why? Using social networks, sending emails with our products and/or services helps people know the name of our company, what we do, what we sell and if we have promotions know what they are. This, while efficient, is impersonal. Calling the person who receives the mail or who is going to receive it explaining who we are, what we offer and what added value we can offer them will help personalize the mail and/or the meeting, and so the prospectus will take us into account. This will make prospects want to read and open our emails and then take us into consideration. Can we improve on cold calling? Of course, we can improve a lot what will help us more prospects want to meet with us, in turn, this will help us have more chances to have more business and increase our income.

What do we recommend? That we begin to practice our techniques of persuasion, it is not easy to convince someone on the phone or call and want to make an appointment. That's why it's important to practice how to persuade prospects to buy our products. How should we talk? It is very important that customers feel our empathy, security, desire to help and that we have a very good deal with them. How do we do this? Speaking calmly, mentioning some problem relevant to them and calling them politely by name. Prospects must trust us, they must trust our product, they must know that we will be able to support them in the event of a problem. You should see us as your friend, but also as a business person, confident in yourself and your product. It is extremely important that they think they are winning and that in the end our product will make their business more profitable than it already is. Prospects should perceive our products with more value than cost.

Do you think cold calling no longer works or are you afraid to make this call? As we have already mentioned, it is very important that you have contact with customers, that you talk to them, that you schedule appointments, that you send them complete information and that you give them the security of knowing what you do as a company and the guarantee of your services and products. Why does this work? Because it is personalized, they can ask you what they need on the phone and they know they will be able to call you in case they have additional doubts or have a problem.

How to convince them or how to show yourself as a business professional? Ask them questions, don't be boring! Most sales executives have the same speech on the phone, think a little outside the box and come up with a type of communication for each customer. What do we mean by that? If you are a slightly younger executive we can make references to topics such as for example some meme of a senior executive, likewise, a senior executive is going to expect a different kind of language. For example, suddenly a junior executive is really interested in having a meeting, but could ask us for a meeting not face-to-face, but via Skype. Be ready! Say yes, have everything at hand, prove that your computer, headphones, internet connection and everything works great. Go to a quiet place, that everything is orderly and although it seems logical, the environment where you have the meeting will affect the perception of the prospect or could initiate a topic of conversation. How? If we are in a dirty office, disordered and with little light, the prospect will not trust us because it is a reflection of how we manage our business and represents us as unreliable. On the other hand, if we have books on our side, everything is tidy, the wall is white for example and not green with red, this will give the prospect the impression that you and your company are trustworthy, that you are an orderly person and that you handle your account very well. Subtle truth?

This type of meetings are important with companies abroad, in case we are going to export our product. If you are a slightly older executive, it is important to take into account how we dress and what the client will expect from us. For example, do not appear in jeans if the prospectus is in an elegant dress or in a suit. Being flexible and with this type of detail, the prospectus will catalogue us as incompatible with your organisation or as a company that does not yet have the size to work with them.

The idea of cold calling is to be able to corroborate that they are really prospects, that we can adapt to your company, that is, that we could work together and have more information about your company in order to have a meeting. For this reason, the questions are important, paying attention to the prospect is important, being able to point the information and keep it in the CRM also adds to our database because apart from collecting we can gather different information that the client has given us on different occasions so we can provide a better proposal. If you're stuck in a prospectus where you're going to call back on a specific day and time, do it! They won't trust you if you don't because they'll be waiting for the call that'll never come. Don't call them another time and apologize, the damage is done. Keep your calendar tidy, you can use Google's calendar, your cell phone's calendar, a planner, a notebook, a calendar or whatever works best for you, but if you need to send some information or call a prospect, do it.

Do you call during office hours? Possibly, you are communicating with the gatekeeper, later we will explain exactly what the gatekeeper is and how to convince it or how it can help us communicate and achieve business with the prospect. Instead of calling the company nine to five, call sooner or later, that could give you a chance that the person answering is the prospect and you can establish a relationship directly with that person.

Chapter 4: Prospecting Techniques

Now that we know what prospecting is and why it's important, start by researching who is in charge of seeing the purchases of the product and/or service you're selling in each company. If you want to have a little more arrival with a contact, look for a friend you have in common to introduce you. If the prospect trusts the person they have in common, he's going to trust you, too. Now, what happens if you don't have any friends in common, no one to contact you? Don't worry, there is no problem, you can contact the prospect in other ways, such as, for example, with cold calls, or you could also present yourself on a professional social network such as LinkedIn. This way, prospects will be able to see your name in the profile, see your credentials, your recommendations, your skills and search for your company as well. For this reason it is very important that your profile is very professional and as detailed as possible. It is also very important that the company's LinkedIn profile has all the necessary information, high quality photos, information on why to use that company, among other information that should be useful for the buyer, such as who we are, how to contact us, success stories, where we are located, among others. It is very important that the company is easy to find on LinkedIn.

On the other hand, we also recommend that you establish credibility in the industry in which you work. How do you do this? Simple, start writing articles, going to networking meetings, commenting on debates and participating in the groups you can, this way, more people will know where you work, what you do, which company you work for and you can be recommended. If people ask for you, they'll know who you are. It is very important that people trust you, that they know that they can call you if they have doubts and that they know that if problems arise, you are going to help them. On the other hand, if you have never spoken on the phone or do not know the product well, we recommend that you have a basic script with the points to mention, this may include warranties, what the product includes, what they can expect, among others. It is better to talk on the phone without a script as it sounds more natural but we always recommend having it so that we do not miss any point that can help us to close a business.

You must remember that not every time you are talking you must sell, you are preparing the bases for the sale and gaining the trust of your customer, it is very important to take this into account so as not to saturate the potential customer. Also, plan your day and use at least forty percent to get in touch and look for new prospects. This will help you expand your network of potential customers and maximize and/or increase your sales. Spend time on social networks, answer questions and comment on your product.

Chapter 5: You need to be looking for prospects 24/7

Why is it so important to be looking for prospects 24/7? I mean, why should we always be looking for prospects? It may seem a bit exaggerated, but the more prospects, the more opportunities for success and the more opportunities we have to meet our goals. Also, the more prospects we look for, the more and better we can relate to more prospects, the more opportunities we have to be recommended and the more opportunities to do business with them. If we have stopped looking for prospects and have relaxed at work, we will notice this in our goals, number of prospects and mainly, in our numbers.

Have you heard about the universal law of necessity? Do you know what it's about? The Universal Law of Necessity dictates that the more you need to sell something, the less likely you are to sell it. I know it seems confusing, but let's get this example straight. Let's say Rodrigo hasn't searched or contacted many prospects during the month, now, he needs to close the different deals, but he's only stayed with a few candidates and has some opportunities. Several of the prospects have already closed deals with their competitors, and now, as the year is coming to an end, they only have a few opportunities they could close. This is going to magnify the Universal Law of Necessity, the more you need to close a deal, the more difficult and less likely you are to do so. Rodrigo is desperate to survive and wants to close these deals anyway. Why should he fail? By the law of attraction. What's the law of attraction got to do with it? If Rodrigo is worried about what will happen if he doesn't reach the goal, he won't think about how to reach the goal, that means that his attention will be focused on surviving and not on how to sell, he will be desperate, he will lose his charisma, the calm, consequently, he will lose these business opportunities, his prospects will hire the competitors and he won't reach his goal. Rodrigo instead of having been busy all year looking for prospects and closing deals to make sure he reached or surpassed his goal, he was relaxed, he trusted himself and now he will be thinking about what to do and what will happen to him when he doesn't reach his goal.

On the other hand, we can talk about Sandra's case, she works looking for prospects every day, looks for contacts to present her, sends emails, schedules meetings and is focused on closing her business. She's organized her time in the best possible way. He arrives, checks his emails, searches for prospects, calls on the phone, verifies again that these prospects he has really talked to are potential clients, schedules meetings, reviews the CRM, personalizes the proposals and practices his presentation. You are always on time for your meetings, check that you have wireless internet, save the presentation on your computer and keep it on an external disk or USB. She's always ready. As she has more business and meets more prospects, her clients also recommend her without even having requested it because she gives them a good personalized service, is always concerned about them and is empathetic. As you have been working hard, you have several prospects, you have almost reached your goal so you are relaxed. This is what customers feel. She knows how to sell her product and knows that even if some prospects sign contracts with competitors, she will reach her goal. He has no rush or desperation to close new deals.

Have you ever heard of the thirty-day law? The law of thirty days dictates that the prospects you have worked for thirty days will bear fruit in the following ninety days; this means that the more prospects you work in a month in a row, that is, the more you work in the year, the more fruit you will get from your work. These could be, for example, commissions earned due to the increase in prospectuses. This will make you arrive at the end of the year more relaxed knowing that, even if some businesses fall and sign with the competition, you have a very good chance of reaching the goal and/or surpassing it. It seems simple, doesn't it? Call different prospects every day, email them, call them back, track them and enjoy the fruits of your work.

Have you ever wondered, why aren't you closing as many sales as you'd like? Have you been making calls, or, are you making the right calls? Really, what is preventing us from working hard and reaching our goals? Is it us? Could it be the lack of tools and strategies, or suddenly, the lack of communication between sales and marketing?

We should start by asking ourselves how much we really like to work, and how are we managing our time? We must perform this analysis, if we are really calling and working our prospects, if we are relaxed, with a positive attitude, practicing our message, personalizing our emails and calls, and giving a clear message to potential customers, we should be closing business. We recommend that in order not to have to be stressed we also understand the law of replacement.

The law of replacement dictates that we must constantly be looking for new prospects in order to replace opportunities that will naturally fail. We must do this according to our ratio, which is equal to or greater than our closing ratio. What do we mean by that? If we have ten prospects and our closing ratio is fifty percent, we know that five prospects will not sign with us. We must therefore look for five more prospects before closing those five contracts so that we can always keep a surplus. This will make it possible for us to achieve our goals and always have more prospects, this can even help us to surpass our goals. Now ask yourself, do you do this in your business? We recommend that you analyze your list, have you kept any records of who you have called in the last month? Do you know the percentage of prospects that close business with you? It is really important that we take these numbers into account and always keep in mind the Universal Law of Necessity, the law of thirty days and our prospect closing ratios. We recommend that you do this exercise after you have finished this book. Check how many prospects you've called, how many meetings you've gotten, and how many businesses they've closed with you. This will make you more objective, what do we mean by that? This will encourage you to look for better prospects, to learn, to differentiate potential customers from people you call who are not necessarily interested in buying our product or service.

Chapter 6: Sales are, and always will be about our numbers

Sales always are and always will be, measured and about our numbers. We have always been measured and our work has always been reflected and measured in our numbers as we come to the end of the month or the date on which we must report. Now, is there any other way to measure our sales? No. How can we measure productivity? With our numbers, how and how much are we selling? How many customers are we calling and how many are we closing business with? How are we organizing our time Are we going to companies to close business? Are we giving away promotional items so customers will remember us? How much are we spending and what percentage are we recovering? Is the type of advertising we are doing worth it? Is it generating results for us? These questions will help us see our real numbers, whether we have a deficit or how much our profit is, whether we are reaching our budget or not, and why. With these questions we can define which direction to take and make the necessary changes to increase our sales. This also helps us understand how much we are spending to find prospects, whether it's on mobility to meet them, on some kind of gift for them, how much we spend on retaining them and how many prospects have become customers. Knowing how much we are spending on our prospects will also give us an idea of whether we should continue spending or what kind of measures we should change.

Our productivity will be reflected in our numbers. The more productive we are in our work, the more prospects we will have, the more appointments we will schedule, therefore, the more clients we will have and our numbers will go up. We must always analyze our numbers, each month we must have a goal that is clear and we must have an annual goal. We have to analyze what our numbers have been from the previous year, and if we have them from the previous year to this one, even better. We must see how we are progressing month by month compared to the previous year. We must measure ourselves in this way, check our numbers weekly, we recommend you to do it especially during the beginning of the week. For example, on Monday we can start by reviewing how our sales are going, the prospects we should call during the day, how our projection is going, how many prospects we should call that day, how many new prospects we should look for and we should know how many sales we should make to achieve our goal, or better yet, to surpass it.

On the other hand, we must always remember that we must take responsibility for reaching our goal. We are responsible for our success or our failures, what we must do is analyse why we have failed, what changes we must make in ourselves or in our procedures, if we have not been motivated or if we have been distracted. What do we mean when we say that we must be responsible for our numbers? This means that we must not blame others for our failures, not the economy, not the policies of our company, not our colleagues, not anyone. We must always have our numbers present, we must remember where to put our efforts and we must self-motivate. With our numbers in mind, not only will we know how far we are from reaching our goal, but we can also take additional measures and this will help us make the necessary changes and adjustments in our strategies and tactics. We can also measure whether the strategies we are using are working. For example, if you have been sending physical mail, emails or have been running social media campaigns, you should measure whether there has been an increase in sales or for example if you have been receiving more inquiries from new prospects about your product. For example, if we have carried out a campaign for people to get to know us, that is, a branding campaign, we must see if the number of prospects has increased, or if the prospects are interested and are calling us to request information about our products. Our numbers should always be our priority, all our indicators should always be kept as high as possible. We must close as much business as we can with our prospects, we must make as many calls and visits as we can. If these numbers are high, our sales and our business will be successful. It's all about working hard and looking for prospects.

Chapter 7: What's stopping you from succeeding?

Have you ever asked yourself this question? What is keeping you from succeeding? What are your habits? What's the first thing you do when you get to the office? Do you pay enough attention to what you're doing all the time? How are your lists? Do you take notes from your customers? Do you call them after you've sent emails? Are you calling them back? How long does it take and how productive are you being? Usually, what prevents us from succeeding and our biggest problem is procrastination. Ask yourself, How much time a day do you spend watching social networks? Reading the news? Are you writing an email, getting distracted, and sending a message to your friend? Are you working and getting distracted with a notification of a social event you've been invited to, or are you responding to a group with your friends at school? Are you trying to get started and keep putting it off for doing something else? So what do we mean by procrastination? This is when you start doing some other activity before you start your work, i.e., or priority. This can be prospecting, sending emails or text messages, that is, instead of putting our hands to work and start what we really have to do, we are watching television, Netflix, reading an article or doing a quiz on the Internet because we find it fun. The typical phrase to know that we are procrastinating is five more minutes, or, in half an hour I start working and that never happens or we work less time than we should in order to be productive.

Procrastinating, in the long run, increases our stress because we will have fewer prospects and we will have to try to close what little we have. Procrastination won't lead to success. Ask yourself, do you always say you're going to do another irrelevant task before you start working and making money? Procrastination is really common, we must analyze why and in what we are procrastinating and find our personal way to stop because it is counterproductive for us. These habits we can and must change to be successful, increase our income and continue to be successful in the business world.

What can we do to avoid procrastinating so much, or rather, how can we stop procrastinating? Let's start by leaving the cell phone in the drawer, leaving it in silence because if we leave it on the vibrator we're going to want to see who wrote us and it's going to tempt us to deconcentrate. It is necessary to deactivate the notifications of the computer in which we are working, among others. This is extremely important if we have Facebook open on the computer, Messenger from the cell phone to the computer, some game or if we have notifications of different pages activities such as a news page. This will also prevent us from falling into the temptation of procrastination. This is going to waste a lot of time and we're not going to be as successful as we could be, in fact, it's not going to allow us to reach and explore our full potential. The next time you find out you're going to procrastinate, stop what you're doing, realize it and start working again. We all need a break from work we know, but your break is to stretch a little back and neck, go for water or prepare a coffee, not to use the cell phone. The problem is that when we start reading an article that has nothing to do with our work or we start playing Candy Crush, we're going to start thinking and focusing our energy on something that won't benefit our success and we're going to have a hard time concentrating and starting over. This will make us lose valuable minutes of work, calls and we may lose business by calling customers late, our competition may already have communicated with them and scheduled a meeting before us and have won the business. Don't get distracted, keep working.

On the other hand, if we are very perfectionist we also tend to take too long or not use the work we have been doing so well, everything seems horrible to us. Additionally, we are going to take too long to perform a simple task, is this worth it? Instead of being prospecting, visiting or sending text messages, we will be stuck in a simple task for too long. This in turn will affect our productivity, our sales and in turn our numbers and the opportunity to reach or better yet, exceed our goal. Everything is related, what we do in a working day directly affects our goals. Have you ever seen it this way before? Have you ever thought about the direct impact of not being focused or writing to our friend? Now, what should we do when we're so perfectionist? How can we handle it? We have to start realizing that our perception is subjective, that we are perfectionists and that that's fine but we have to improve in this aspect in order to increase our productivity. Perfectionists tend to focus a lot on the final product rather than the process. We must focus on both, so we can search and find out where it is and what we can offer prospects as an added value of our products and/or services. It's also very important to have fun while we're creating. Leave perfectionism aside, try to do things as best as possible, but you need to set a time limit, or deadline, to be able to perform the tasks in the time we set.

Now, we have to think, what happens when we're demoralized, when we're not selling? We tell you that paralysis is real and this happens when we have stopped doing some activity and it is difficult for us to start again, when we are demoralized. For example, many writers stop writing and feel that they have failed, find it hard to start over because they feel that they are not good enough or that they cannot start, that they will never be as creative as the other person and that they do not have enough potential, that is, they feel as if they are losers. They have what's known as the "writer's block." Did it happen to you? Do you feel identified? To have confidence in ourselves is not an easy process, just like getting out of this paralysis, it is going to cost us effort, but we must do it. For these reasons it is very important to be careful with the three "P's". Procrastination, perfectionism and paralysis. When we fall into one, it is very difficult to get out, and if we fall into the three even more complicated. We must always be aware of what we are doing and have the three "p's" present.

For paralysis we must realize that we can take as long as it takes to be able to start over. In other words, instead of being frustrated, we should give ourselves permission to take the time necessary to be able to start again. If we get frustrated it's going to be worse because we're not going to be able to do any activity, we're going to stress more, and that's not going to help us start over and be productive. If we want, we can carry out different activities that could help us to start creating again, for example, suddenly we recommend to change the place of work, in the sense that, if we always work in a certain place, we look for another one that inspires us more. Let's change the place, the desk, the view, the schedule, also the work. Many people are more productive in the morning and there are other people who are more productive at night. If we must make calls, they should not always be in the hours of nine to five, may be earlier or later, take this into account in a schedule that is non-invasive to the customer. If we know that we are blocked and have not been concentrating on the morning, let's take advantage of the night to advance our reports and not waste time making them the next day, let's follow the schedule and the most important thing is that we complete the tasks that we have proposed that day.

We can also try different things, suddenly we can put some kind of music to help us create or concentrate, music that has no lyrics, just melody, for example. On the other hand, we can also start practicing some sport or doing any kind of activity that helps us to get out of our comfort zone so that we can start our work again and be inspired again. It's really important that we trust ourselves, that we don't feel disappointed and that we understand that these processes take time. Take a deep breath and start the process all over again! Start creating with peace of mind and without judging yourself. This will improve the quality of the work and make us feel more at ease. If we fail, it is important that we can and know that we can always start over. If we want to be successful, we must go forward so that we encounter adversity along the way, no one who has achieved success has had an easy path.

Success is not easy, you must look for different ways to stay motivated and stay on track that is not always easy, because there are many times when we want to throw in the towel and we think it is the only way out we have. We must remember and emphasize that customers can perceive what we are feeling and that our emotions directly affect our work, that is, our business and therefore our ability to succeed. We must learn to fight procrastination, have different rituals before we work to be more creative, follow our plans and our schedules. The most important thing is to realize what our employers are and work on them, we can motivate ourselves in different ways, the most important thing is not to give up and follow the path of success.

Chapter 8: Time Management is the Key

Time management is key to our success, it will contribute to our success or failure. Time is money, it's super important that we understand this. Now, you must analyze how you are distributing your time? What are you doing all day? Do you feel like you are missing hours in the day? What do you do in twenty-four hours? Analyze what activities you are doing and how long each one takes. It is very important that we have a schedule with the activities to perform and how long each should take, if not, we can fall back into procrastination. A planned day is more effective than a drifting day. We can and should already have the list of which clients we are going to call and have as much information as possible of this contact, we must know if we are going to advance some promotion, how much time we need to be able to carry out our planning of our clients, if we are going to look for more prospects that day, among others.

A really important aspect of the job is being able to take responsibility and accept our successes and failures. It is very important that we always have and maintain the right mentality, what do we mean by this? That we bear in mind that failures are opportunities in which we can learn, adjust our proposals, procedures, learn and start over. We should not be ashamed of our failures, it is the way we can learn and we can improve. Analyzing our failures and managing them will lead to success. Let us be proud of both our achievements and our failures. Keep in mind that many times we will want to do other things besides looking for prospects, we are going to get bored because it is not easy, nor is it easy to have to plan our calls or do research, but it is very important to always keep in mind that this is the most important activity and should be our priority.

So, if we have so many activities, how can we always prioritize our prospects? You must learn to delegate tasks that take time from someone else who could do them. How many people do you have on your team? Do you know what each person's talents are? Their strengths? Start paying attention and start delegating tasks that take up your time and could be done by someone on your team. You will see how they strive to do these tasks well because you are trusting them and giving them more responsibility. This will also make the office productivity also start to increase, change a little the daily routine and give more responsibility, is a good way to increase productivity and show that you trust your team. In this way you also have less work, less burden, do not move away from your focus which is looking for prospects and do not leave tasks unfulfilled. By combining the strengths of the office, you can boost your business.

We can't help but mention the Hortsmans Colorarium, have you heard of it? Let us begin by explaining what we mean and what points we should remember according to the Corollary of Hortsmans. It is very important that we bear in mind the following key principles. Here we go, it's all about the people you work with, spend time with them, learn as much as you can from them and pay attention, if they have children, their strengths, their weaknesses and what they are passionate about. People can overcome and improve mediocre systems, but mediocre systems will never be able to improve people's work. The more communication you have with your team, the better. It doesn't matter if you are having a bad day, the more and better communication you have with your employees and collaborators, the more confident they will be to communicate what is happening and to ask specialized questions in case they need it. They will try harder if they have a better relationship with you, they will have the confidence to ask you the questions they need, or if they have a problem with a potential client, they will be able to tell you about it and solve it instead of losing the prospect.

Let's continue, another principle of the Hortsmans Corollary is also to take into account that you cannot deceive people, people realize when you are hiding the truth or when you are giving them false information. It is very important to always communicate with our colleagues and with our prospects and customers and to be honest with them about what is going on. We must remember that we are not in control of anything, that this is impossible and that we are not going to be able to have it. It is very important that you build relationships based on trust, not only with your prospects but also with your collaborators. This is what will let you influence people and even if you don't agree, you can trust the decisions of your team and they will trust yours. Don't forget to remember that sometimes people won't be able to meet the established dates, not everything must be in the exact time, sometimes, there are times when they won't be able to meet, but that shouldn't say that you will be able to punish your team for that. You have to be a little flexible and understand that an organization is made up of people who like you, are learning and will have good and bad days, this is completely normal, we must accept it.

Another very important and worth emphasizing principle is that you can't keep secrets, everything comes to light. Why is it important to mention this point, because your team must trust you and working together will be able to make better decisions. It is important that they too are informed and can contribute to your company's current situation. Another principle we must practice and understand is that how we feel is our fault, that is, it is our responsibility to be able to manage our emotions and to be able to change our feelings and perspective of a meeting. What do we mean by this? That we have to learn to control how we react to different situations. It is very important to understand why this situation was created and how it can be solved. The reaction you have is much more powerful than you think. Remember that we must be the example to follow, that emotional intelligence is key to success. Our team follows our steps, they must see us as respectable and stable people, they must follow our example, they must always see us calm, serene, positive, they must know that we are analytical, that we know where we are going. They can't see us losing our temper, that's not good. They must see that, in all situations, no matter how complicated, we always remain calm and look for different solutions. The important thing is to be able to solve and be able to improve in order to become successful people.

It should be noted that our way of doing things is not the only one, many people have been successful and have not done things in the same way as us. Learn to be open with people, learn to listen to ideas and try new techniques and strategies. Why not? What do we have to lose? We have to take the risk, if a particular strategy is not working, let us try a new one, let us be flexible, let us be open to treating things differently, this is the real road to success. Also, in order to achieve our goals we must avoid losing concentration. How often are we checking the cell phone, looking out the window or thinking about anything but what we should really be doing? Why is it important to maintain concentration? Because the more we deconcentrate, the more time we lose producing, looking for prospects, the longer it takes us to refocus, and the road to success is going to be longer.

It is very important that we know what our habits are and how we procrastinate, we must analyze everything, this has already been mentioned, this is linked to procrastination. Let's check our office or the place where we work. What distracts us? Do we have WhatsApp on the computer? Do we have the Nintendo Switch on our side and want to play? What do we need to be able to stop distracting ourselves? Suddenly closing the office door, not having our cell phone or our tablet on the side. Distraction subtracts our productivity and does not allow us to reach our goal at the rate we could or our potential. We have to realize when we're getting distracted and start over. Little by little, we'll stop getting distracted. This will be reflected in our numbers. When we start increasing our leads, when we start closing deals with customers, when we get more commissions, we'll be more motivated and we'll realize how much time we've really been wasting.

Now, how do we focus on our tasks? Are there people around you? Are they listening to music too loud or talking too loud? Tell them that you need a couple of hours without interruptions, in case something urgent is needed, you will be able to attend to them, but if it is something that could wait ask them for that time. Is your office very noisy? Work in another place where there is no noise or interruptions, close your door, go to a café, anywhere where you can concentrate and you will not be interrupted. On the other hand, if you have a corporate email or use programs like Skype for Business, put in your busy state, this will prevent people from interrupting you. You can put a message of automatic answer that says that you will be available from certain hour so that at that moment they can ask you what they need. It is also very important to disable notifications as they distract us. That message from WhatsApp,

Facebook Messenger, Instagram or social network notifications distracts us if we don't think so.

When we are focused on a task, listening to the vibrating cell phone decentralizes us and we waste at least a couple of minutes getting back to what we were doing. Imagine if your cell phone vibrated every ten minutes and it took you five minutes to concentrate again because you wanted to see who was writing to you, or if someone put Like to what you hung up, if they responded to the e-mail you had sent, how much time do you waste in an hour? Worse yet, how much time do you waste all day? We must make the most of twenty-four hours a day, and wasting time in this way is not productive. However, we must have a planned time a day to be able to review our emails or social networks. It is very important that we are able to respond to customers in a timely manner. Verify what works best for you. You could check your inbox in the morning when you wake up, after lunch and before you leave the office. This will increase your productivity and you won't leave any mail unanswered, the most important thing is that you will be able to respond quickly to your prospects and potential customers.

On the other hand, it is very important that we know and learn to calculate our value. What are we good at? Have we been trained in a specific area? How can we contribute to our company? Can we review processes and improve them? Are we contributing as much as we can to our company? We must evaluate our strengths, weaknesses and see how we can improve. The most important thing is to recognize our value. Stay focused so that your productivity increases, to improve your sales, to have more prospects, to have a good business and to be successful. Are you already seeing how small details, changes in your routine and how changing our organization is changing and increasing your opportunity to be successful? A habit is created in twenty-one days, during this time follow everything to the letter, you will see how easy and how quickly you get used to these new habits.

Chapter 9: Prospectus Goals

It is very important for us to have contact and make the first contact with our prospects. To remember, prospects are potential customers who might be interested in using our products and/or services, we know this because they are aligned with our target market. To make contact with our prospects it is very important to do a little research first. Do we have a friend in common with the prospect? How are we going to contact the prospect of a company? Can we call and ask for the person in charge? Is it better to call and introduce ourselves on the company's website? Do we send an email and call to introduce ourselves? After the first presentation which can be virtual or by phone, it is important that we ask the prospect for a meeting. It is different to explain all the information and benefits of purchasing our product and/or company by phone than in person.

We must also investigate our prospect, know what his profile is. This will help us not only to know what kind of information to bring but also to understand how to sell them. On the other hand, we can also realize that it is not worth spending our time with them because they are not real prospects. This is going to waste time and money when we could be investing both in another prospect who could become our client. It is very important to know the motivation of our prospects, what they need, what we can offer them as an added value and what they like. This prior research will allow us to assemble a presentation that is molded to your needs. Also, once they know you, it's easier to be contacted or recommended.

Keep in mind that we must be very professional at the time of introduction, we must bring all our material ready and be as short and accurate as possible. After this, it is very important to know when to call them, if we know we have a friend in common, we should ask them to introduce us. It is very important to know in what kind of situation they are going to present us, clearly, that they present us in a social party with a lot of noise is not going to be so efficient and it is preferable that they present us in another type of situation.

Now, after having researched the customer's needs and having presented our services and/or products according to them, we must close the sale. It is very important to be clear from the beginning with the cost, you do not have to have any hidden costs. We must also be clear about the contract, cancellation policies, among others. Honesty will lead us to maintain and create better customer relationships and have better recommendations. In order to build a good relationship we must listen to the client consciously, many times a client is talking to us and we are thinking about something else and the client notices it. It is important for the client to know that we are paying attention. Similarly, it is important to know the name of the client, we should always address them with respect and for their name.

Equally, it is important to be flexible but formal in all situations. We must always remember that no matter how much trust we have and even if they treat us informally, we must always maintain composure and formalism to some extent. We must never forget to speak with a smile, that conveys confidence and happiness. If we're smiling, that helps us build trust and a better relationship with our customer. It is very important to be empathic with them, to put ourselves in their position in order to understand them and to offer them solutions or alternatives that are compatible for the prospects. It also shows that we care about them and can anticipate questions or concerns.

Many clients despair or suddenly are having a bad day, and it is very important to let them complain or tell us everything they have to say without interrupting them and once they are calmer or quieter try to explain or help them in what they need. This way they'll feel like we're supporting them. We must emphasize the importance that we can never lose our papers with them, interrupt them, raise our voice or worse, hang up the phone. Our language is really important, how we respond, how we address customers, how we sit among others. There are negative phrases that we say without realizing it, for example, instead of saying "I don't know" it is better to answer "don't worry, I'll find out and send you the answer". We must also be careful how we sit, whether we cross our arms, whether we are sitting upright, realise this and consider how best to sit. Our position influences the perception of our client. For example, if we are sitting with our arms crossed, in a rather relaxed posture almost lying on the chair, the client will think we don't care. It is important that we sit straight and a little bit towards the client so that they see that we are attentive, paying attention and that we want to be there.

Chapter 10: The Pyramid of Prospects

It is very important that we take into account the pyramid of prospects, let's start with a practical and simple example. When you walk into the office, who is the first person you call? The first person on your list? Why? Where do you get the list? The list must be properly worked, if the contacts are the ones you are downloading from your database, it is time to make changes. Remember that a prospect is not the same as a contact, a prospect is a potential client. At the top of the pyramid is the smallest group, usually one percent of your customer base, they are the prospects who are ready to buy, they may have a contract with another company that is expiring and we know they are ready to renew it and have the budget. This group is the most lucrative, in this group we must spend more time and energy. We must meet, all our mail must be personalized, we must accommodate their schedules and adapt to what they need.

Then we find clients who also demand your great attention, usually is four percent of your client portfolio, after this, we have a medium group that is usually fifteen percent of the total. This gives us a twenty percent total that are our prospects and our most important customers. We must focus most of our time and energy on them, adjust to them, call them, and schedule meetings. After this group we have the largest group which are the rest of the prospects, but in which we should not spend so much time and energy, but we should take them into account. With this information, we must now revisit our list taking into account the pyramid of prospects, reorganize our calls and re-evaluate our prospects.

Conclusion

In order to start looking for prospects we must start by understanding what a prospect is. Prospects are potential customers who are interested and would be willing to buy our product. We must learn to separate them, understand what kind of prospect they are and how to deal with them. We must also understand and understand that we ourselves with the habits we have acquired over the years can be avoiding and boycotting our own success. We must stop procrastinating, among other habits that prevent us from succeeding. We invite you to read our following volumes so that you can learn and succeed in business. We must stop being afraid, we must throw ourselves into our project and trust that we can achieve it. Volume II and Volume III will help you achieve success in the business world, we will give you all the strategies and tools you need to build relationships with prospects, have networking and give different tactics to be successful in the business world.

Glossary

Prospectus: A potential client is a person or company with whom we have no business relationship but whose interests could make him a client. Today's prospect is tomorrow's customer.

Segmentation: Segmentation divides a market into smaller segments of buyers who have different needs, characteristics and behaviors that require differentiated marketing strategies or mixes. For example, we can segment our prospects, i.e. potential customers, prospects in the CRM, among others.

Emailing: Sending emails to several emails simultaneously oriented specifically to sell. This allows us to retain, build loyalty, send promotions and important information to our customers. We can have several different mailing lists.

Cold calling: Make calls to potential customers.

CRM: Program that helps Customer Management in an organized way.

Gatekeeper: A person within a company or organization, usually a management executive or executive assistant. This person is valuable because he or she can influence the prospect's decision. In this case, we must know how to deal with it. They usually know what the organization's problems are and our product could also simplify their work.

Linkedin: It is a professional social network for companies and where normal people can put information about where we work, what has been our education, experience, skills and qualities. Additionally, we can certify with the new LinkedIn certificates. We can have LinkedIn on our Android and IOS operating systems or on the computer.

Networking

Facebook: Social network where we can communicate with different people in different parts of the world. It is a way to share content in a simple and fast way on the Internet. It is available for the Android and IOS operating systems.

Instagram: Social network and application. Its function is to upload photos, videos and stories. It's available for Android and iOS devices.

The Universal Law of Necessity: The University of Necessity law dictates that the more you need to sell something, the less likely you are to sell it. I know it seems confusing, but let's get this example straight. Let's just say that Rodrigo hasn't searched or contacted many prospects during the month, now, he needs to close contacts but he just stayed and has some opportunities.

Law of thirty days: Law of thirty days dictates that the prospects you have worked for thirty days will bear fruit in the following ninety days; this means that the more prospects you work in a month in a row, that is, the more you work in the year, the more fruits, call for example commissions you will get due to the increase in prospects.

Procrastination: This is when you do another activity instead of actually doing what you are supposed to be doing.

Perfectionism: Perfectionists also tend to take too long or not use the work we've been doing so well; everything seems horrible to us. Additionally, we are going to take too long to perform a simple task, is this worth it?

Paralysis: it is real and this happens when we have stopped doing some activity and it tells us to start again. For example, many writers stop writing and feel that they have failed, find it hard to start over because they feel that they are not good enough or that they cannot start, that they will never be as creative as the other person and that they do not have enough potential, that is, they feel as if they are losers.

Corollary of Hortsmans: Principles to be taken into account in order to achieve better sales, more productivity in the team and more success.

Social Selling: Social Selling is a sales model in which we use different social media, giving priority to LinkedIn.

What we are implementing is a form of customer attraction based on branding, human relationships and developing useful content for our potential customers.

B2B: Business to business or company to company.

Gatekeeper: A person within a corporation who can influence the purchase of a product. They work closely with the decision maker. You could be an assistant and most likely you know your boss's problems and have to deal with them, so getting your product will benefit them too.

Influencer: Now, we have another type of person in the organization who can help us sell our product and have a successful meeting with the decision maker, these people usually have a Junior level and compare the products and their characteristics to see what is most beneficial to the company. This person can be categorized under the name of influencer, they do not make the decision directly, just as their opinion has weight and can influence the sale.

Toxic Influencer: People who impersonate an influence but are not. They will usually say that they have a good position in the company, that they have a good relationship with their superiors, that they earn a lot of money and that they have a lot of money. They're gonna give out a lot of information without us asking for it.

Trigger Event: It is an event that can generate sales. For example, a prospect changed company and this appears on LinkedIn. How does it impact our company? It could generate a window for a sale in the new company where you are working and could generate an additional sale in the old company.

Google Alerts: These are alerts that we can configure in Google so that we receive different news depending on what we configure. For example, each time there is a press release, an alert will be sent to the cell phone or device we have configured.

Citation (APA Style)

1) Beatriz Soto, B. S. (2018a, 17 October). What is mailing? Discover everything related to the sending of massive mails. Retrieved October 5, 2019, from https://www.gestion.org/que-es-el-mailing/

2) Carlo Farucci, C. F. (n.d.). How to calculate #ROI in #MarketingDigital? Retrieved October 5, 2019, from https://josefacchin.com/roi-retorno-de-inversion/

3) Definition of prospection - Definicion.de. (n.d.). Retrieved October 5, 2019, from https://definicion.de/prospeccion/

4) Douglas Burdett, D. B. (s.f.). Sales Prospecting Without Social Media Is Like Selling Without a Phone. Recuperado 5 octubre, 2019, de https://www.salesartillery.com/blog/sales-prospecting-social-media-selling

5) Fanatical Prospecting: The Ultimate Guide to Opening Sales Conversations and Filling the Pipeline by Leveraging Social Selling, Telephone, Email, Text, and Cold Calling. (s.f.). Recuperado 5 octubre, 2019, de https://www.oreilly.com/library/view/fanatical-prospecting-the/9781119144755/20_chapter12.html

6) Jesús L. Cortiñas, J. L. C. (2016, 27 April). Is the prospect...? - Management Notes. Retrieved October 5, 2019, from https://www.apuntesgestion.com/b/la-prospeccion-es/

7) Jonathan Ebenstein, J. E. (2016, 28 abril). 5 tips for leveraging your CRM data. Recuperado 5 octubre, 2019, de https://www.bizjournals.com/bizjournals/how-to/marketing/2016/04/5-tips-for-leveraging-your-crm-data.html

8) Josh Slone, J. S. (2019, 27 septiembre). Cold Calling Techniques That Actually Work – Gist. Recuperado 5 octubre, 2019, de https://getgist.com/cold-calling-techniques-that-actually-work/

9) Krishna Srinivas, K. S. (2018, 23 octubre). 12 Techniques to Write a Sales Prospecting Email that Surely Gets Responses. Recuperado 5 octubre, 2019, de https://blog.klenty.com/prospecting-email-sales/

10) The 8 most useful prospecting methods for your company. (2019a, 9 July). Retrieved October 5, 2019, from https://clickbalance.com/blog/contabilidad-y-administracion/metodos-de-prospeccion/

11) The 8 most useful prospecting methods for your company. (2019b, July 9). Retrieved October 5, 2019, from

https://clickbalance.com/blog/contabilidad-y-administracion/metodos-de-prospeccion/

12) MC Donald, D. E. V. O. N. (2010, 16 septiembre). Outbound Prospecting Defined | OpenView. Recuperado 5 octubre, 2019, de https://openviewpartners.com/blog/outbound -prospecting-defined/

13) Nicole Mertes, N. M. (2019, 6 septiembre). Traditional Prospecting vs. Inbound Prospecting. Recuperado 5 octubre, 2019, de https://www.weidert.com/whole_brain_market ing_blog/traditional-prospecting-vs.-inbound-prospecting

14) NIDKEL, A. N. (2017, 25 mayo). The Hub and Spoke Model for Marketing: The Wheel is Still King | CNP. Recuperado 5 octubre, 2019, de https://cnpagency.com/blog/the-hub-and-spoke-model-for-marketing-the-wheel-is-still-king/

15) Olga Milevska, O. M. (2019, 4 julio). What is Prospecting? Definition and Best Methods to Get More Customers. Recuperado 5 octubre, 2019, de https://www.crazycall.com/blog/sales-prospecting-methods

16) PADILLA, R. P. (n.d.). Prospection of Clients: Learn How to Do It Right. Retrieved October 5, 2019, from https://www.genwords.com/blog/prospeccion -de-clientes

17) Paul S. Goldner, P. S. G. (n.d.). Hot Prospecting - customer acquisition. Retrieved October 5, 2019, from https://www.leadersummaries.com/resumen/prospeccion-en-caliente

18) Paula McKinney, P. M. (n.d.). Text Messaging Your Network Marketing Prospect. Retrieved October 5, 2019, from https://paula-mckinney.com/text-messaging-network-marketing-prospect/

19) Press office, P. O. (2019, 22 May). 6 tips to get the most out of your CRM - redk ES. Retrieved October 5, 2019, from https://www.redk.net/es-ES/blog/crm-6-consejos-aprovechar-maximo/

20) Sales prospection | Socialetic. (2013, 17 December). Retrieved October 5, 2019, from https://www.socialetic.com/prospeccion-de-ventas.html

21) What is CRM: Customer Relationship Management and CRM Software. (s.f.-a). Retrieved October 5, 2019, from https://www.sumacrm.com/soporte/que-es-crm

22) What is CRM: Customer Relationship Management and CRM Software. (s.f.-b). Retrieved October 5, 2019, from https://www.sumacrm.com/soporte/que-es-crm

23) What the client and your prospects want. (2012, 14 December). Retrieved October 5, 2019, from

http://blog.brainstormer.es/que-quiere-el-cliente-y-tus-prospectos/

24) Sarah Kathleen Peck, S. K. P. (2018, 7 junio). The Art of Asking: Or, How to Ask And Get What You Want. Recuperado 5 octubre, 2019, de https://medium.com/startup-pregnant/the-art-of-asking-or-how-to-ask-and-get-what-you-want-9e7455ca375b

25) Shane Barker, S. B. (2019, 2 octubre). 7 Simple Ways to Drive Sales on Social Media (With Examples). Recuperado 5 octubre, 2019, de https://medium.com/better-marketing/7-simple-ways-to-drive-sales-on-social-media-with-examples-8012193aa2fb

26) SONIA DURIO LIMIA, S. D. L. (n.d.) What is Social Selling and how can it make you sell more? Retrieved October 5, 2019, from https://josefacchin.com/social-selling-que-es/

27) Tom Smith, T. O. M. (2014, 14 febrero). 8 Benefits of Customer Relationship Management Software. Recuperado 5 octubre, 2019, de http://www.insightsfromanalytics.com/blog/bid/374342/8-benefits-of-customer-relationship-management-software

28) WENDY CONNICK, W. C. (2019, 31 julio). Meaning of WIIFM in Sales Keeping Prospect's Needs Top of Mind. Recuperado 5 octubre, 2019, de https://www.thebalancecareers.com/what-is-wiifm-2917381

29) How to assemble the best customer prospecting strategy? (2018, 7 December). Retrieved October 5, 2019, from https://blog.hotmart.com/es/prospeccion-de-clientes/

30) What is segmentation in marketing? LCMK. (2019, 12 March). Retrieved October 5, 2019, from https://laculturadelmarketing.com/que-es-segmentar-en-marketing/

31) What is a CRM? Understands what a CRM is and what it offers to the different areas of a company. (n.d.). Retrieved October 5, 2019, from https://www.elegircrm.com/crm/que-es-un-crm

www.ingramcontent.com/pod-product-compliance
Lightning Source LLC
Chambersburg PA
CBHW050525190326
41458CB00045B/6709/J